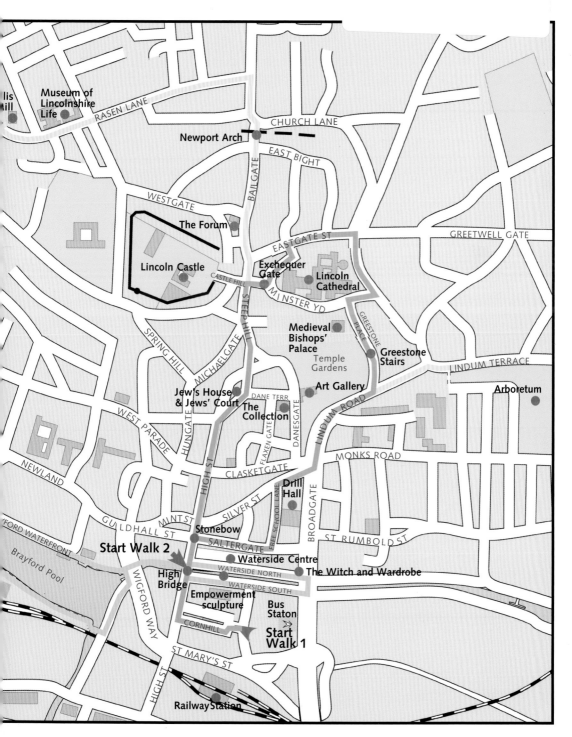

Welcome to Lincoln

Few cities can present as dramatic a profile as Lincoln.
From many miles away, the cathedral on its ridge
makes a thrilling silhouette high above the surrounding landscape. Closer to, its mighty Gothic towers
dominate the city's rooftops. Nearer still, and Lincoln's
ancient castle is seen to share the heights, less spectacular perhaps but, like its ecclesiastical counterpart, still
a real source of power today. Lincoln is a city of two
halves: the historic citadel above and, below, the commercial hub, with an earlier history of its own. Linking
the two is High Street, one of Britain's best-preserved
streets, uniting the city not only with itself but with
its past. What better way for today's visitor to explore,
experience and enjoy this beautiful city?

A short history

For thousands of years, water was the chief mode of transport. The pool where two rivers joined to pierce the limestone ridge on their way to the sea was a focus for river activity. Iron Age folk settled here. Around AD 50 the Romans came, building a wooden fortress on the hill. From the pre-Roman *lindon* – the place by the pool – they called it 'Lindum'. South of the pool, two Roman highways met: Ermine Street from London and the Fosse Way from Exeter and the Midlands. Ermine Street, continuing on its way to York, went arrow-straight through the town, its route still represented, approximately, by the line of High Street. In AD 80 the Romans founded a *colonia*, a town for retired legionaries – these days *Lindum Colonia* has become Lincoln. But by 410, the Romans had gone.

In the next shadowy centuries, invaders sailed from Continental coastlands to settle in eastern England, first Angles and Saxons, then Danes. Agriculture thrived, trade boomed and Lincoln became a wealthy inland fortress-port. Then came the Normans. In 1068 William the Conqueror ordered that a castle be built. Four years later a mighty cathedral was begun, transformed in the 12th century after fire and earthquake into a Gothic marvel. Down by the pool, Lincoln's cloth trade soared. It was not to last: the Black Death (1348), Boston's rivalry and Cromwell's cannon (1644–8) all caused the city to suffer grievously.

In the 1700s gradual revival took place, but it was the coming of the railways in the 1840s which saw Lincoln really take off once more. Engineering for agriculture led to engineering for war – notably William Foster's tank, first developed here, and the Ruston company's engines. Now this too has declined, but today Lincoln has a new identity as a university city and cultural centre.

High Bridge

With a few minor deviations, Lincoln's High Street follows the line of Roman Ermine Street, traditionally linking the commercial area by the waterside to the military, ecclesiastical and administrative headquarters on the hill. For almost 2,000 years, therefore, it has been the focus of city life.

High Bridge

Built around 1160 at the point where High Street crosses the River Witham, High Bridge is the oldest bridge in Britain to have buildings actually constructed on it. Soon after being built, it was extended east to accommodate a chapel in memory of the martyred archbishop Thomas Becket, which stood here until 1763. In medieval times the bridge became the city's main point for meat and fish trading. The river here is shallow, however, preventing larger boats getting through. It was only the cost of demolition that saved the bridge from being pulled down in 1803.

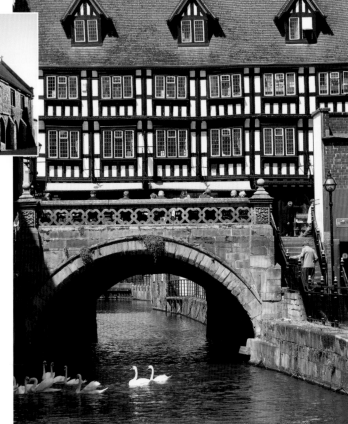

Greyfriars   *High Bridge*

Greyfriars

Greyfriars, almost hidden behind St Swithin's Church, is a rare survival from one of the city's four medieval friaries. This long stone building was built in the 13th century as the church of a huge Franciscan friary. At that time, the friary stretched north from the banks of the River Witham as far as Silver Street.

The Stonebow

The river once flowed past this fine stone arch, and the remains of the old Roman south gate, which it replaced, lie beneath it. The Stonebow is Lincoln's natural meeting place and gets its name from the Scandinavian stennibogi, meaning stone arch. It is mainly 15th-century, although not completed until 1520. It has since been modified, especially in the 19th century, but retains most of its original features.

Stonebow statue

The Posy Ring

Since 1852, incoming mayors of Lincoln have been ceremonially 'married' to the city by putting on a gold posy ring that dates from 1578. An inch (2.5 cm) in diameter, the ring is placed on the new mayor's thumb at the Annual Meeting of the Council. The ring is on display with other council insignia in the old Debtors' Prison at the Guildhall.

Guildhall

Linked to the Stonebow, the Guildhall has been for many centuries where the city's administrators meet. Ceremonial meetings are still held here. In medieval times it was the merchant guilds that ruled through an assembly known as the burwarmote. The City Council followed, called to meetings since the 1370s by the Mote Bell, on the south side of the Stonebow. Until the later 18th century, the city gaol was here, with dungeons for criminals and street-level cells for debtors.

The Stonebow

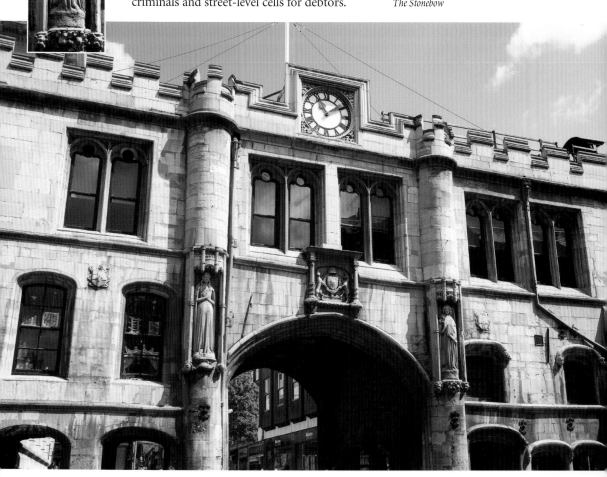

Steep Hill

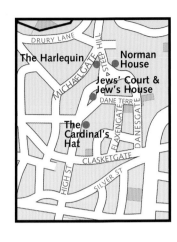

The Steep Hill area, at one time called Mikelgate, was once the centre of a thriving Jewish community. Three of its best-known buildings, the Jew's House, Jews' Court and the Norman House, have particular Jewish connections. In the Middle Ages, fairs and Lincoln's various markets – fish, poultry, corn, meat – were held on certain weekdays up and down the hill.

The Cardinal's Hat and Dernstall House

Look out for these two fine half-timbered houses on your right as you climb the hill. On the corner of Grantham Street is the 15th-century Cardinal's Hat, named after Henry VIII's famous Lord Chancellor, Thomas Wolsey (c.1475–1530), who was first Dean, then Bishop, of Lincoln. At the start of The Strait is Dernstall House, which has masonry within dating from the 12th century.

The Jew's House

This famous building is one of the oldest surviving domestic dwellings in the country. Built around 1150, the house was almost certainly occupied by a merchant who would have lived upstairs and traded downstairs. One name linked with ownership is Belaset of Wallingford, a woman executed in 1287, possibly on a trumped-up charge, for clipping coin – paring the edges of coins to acquire illicit gold and silver.

Jews' Court

Jews' Court, these days the headquarters of the county's historical society, was built much later than the house next door. Very probably it takes its name from a synagogue said to have been situated nearby.

The Jew's House and Jews' Court

The Jews in Lincoln

During the 11th and 12th centuries Lincoln was very prosperous, largely through its wool trade. The Jewish community played a big part in the city's development, especially as money-lenders – an occupation forbidden to Christians. Jews even helped fund the building of the cathedral. However their wealth and the fervour of the Crusades inspired resentment. Persecution in 1266 was followed by expulsion in 1290. Many saw this as an opportunity to rid themselves of their debts.

The Harlequin and Steep Hill

Norman House

Built somewhere between 1170 and 1190, the Norman House is one of the earliest stone houses on Steep Hill. The rounded Romanesque arch of the doorway is typical of its period. Nearby, on opposite sides of the street, are two stones marking the boundary between the juris-diction of the city council and the castle constable. City dwellers had to be gone by sunset. Further up, a magnificent Roman gateway once stood, with double carriageway and side arches. Some of its stonework is still visible at No. 44.

The Harlequin

The half-timbered Harlequin at the junction of Steep Hill and Michaelgate was built in the 15th century. For most of its life it was a public house, the favoured inn for artistes appearing at a theatre that was opened in 1744 in nearby Drury Lane.

Norman House

The Cardinal's Hat

Castle Hill

Castle Hill, often known as Castle Square, embodies 2,000 years of history. For almost a millennium it represented the axis of power in the city, between castle and cathedral. Before that it was where Roman Ermine Street breasted the ridge on its way to the original Lindum Colonia (see page 12), a few hundred metres away. Today, Castle Hill is the site of Lincoln's famous Christmas Market.

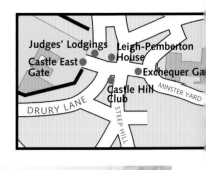

East Gate

Castle East Gate

The East Gate was once the main entrance to the castle, a drawbridge originally guarding the main way across the surrounding ditch. In the 14th century two towers were added to create a barbican, an outward projection of the gate, replacing the drawbridge. The unfortunate invader who penetrated the first gate found himself trapped in a high, narrow stone-walled canyon, where he could be subjected to murderous fire from all angles. Today, cobblestone circles indicate the position of the two towers, demolished to permit construction of the Judges' Lodgings in 1810.

Castle Hill

The Judges' Lodgings

This imposing building constructed of local yellow brick was designed by William Hayward in 1809 to accommodate the judges who came every quarter to try cases at the Crown Court within the castle. The stone pediment above the front door displays the Hanoverian royal coat of arms. The building still fulfils its original purpose, these days housing travelling High Court judges, but also helps pay for its keep by acting as an upmarket wedding venue.

Leigh-Pemberton House

This timber-framed house, built in 1543, is roughly on the line of the old Roman road. Originally owned by a merchant, it possibly became an inn, the Ironmonger's Arms, in the 17th century, but for most of the last century the building served as a bank. It was presented to the city of Lincoln by Bank of England Governor Sir Robin Leigh-Pemberton. This well-preserved Tudor building is now home to the Tourist Information Centre.

Leigh-Pemberton House

Castle Hill Club

Built in the 18th century, many executioners stayed here. Most famous was William Marwood (1820–83) who, through grisly experiments on sheep and dogs, discovered a technique for instantaneous, relatively painless hanging, based on varying the length of drop according to the weight of the victim.

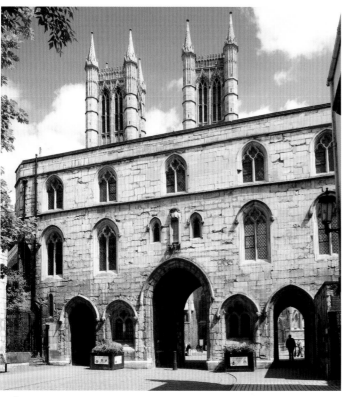

Exchequer Gate

Exchequer Gate

The Church has traditionally owned much land and buildings, and Exchequer Gate was where tenants of old came to pay their rents. Counting was made easier by a table with squares on it – a check pattern – hence the word exchequer.

Christmas Market

From its origins with 12 stalls in 1982, Lincoln's four-day Christmas Market has become the largest in Europe, with over 300 stalls spread throughout the Cathedral Quarter. It was inspired by the one held in Neustadt, Germany, which is Lincoln's twin town. Over 250,000 people come to the city to enjoy the market each year.

Lincoln Castle

Lincoln's castle was established by William the Conqueror in 1068 as a seat of royal power. His architects put it roughly where the Romans had built their timber fortress, using the old walls as its outer bailey. The first Norman fort was also of wood, built on an earth bank and surrounded by a deep ditch – not a moat, for the limestone wouldn't have held water. In later centuries, stone replaced timber, and the castle saw many battles during the Middle Ages, changing hands several times. Cromwell's soldiers besieged it and put paid to it as a fortress, and it became simply the focus of local government, law and order.

Observatory Tower

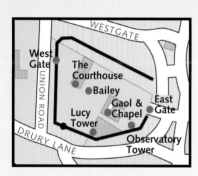

Observatory Tower

Governor of the prison John Merryweather (1768–1862) had the tower made higher in 1822. Although ostensibly built to watch for prison breakouts, the tower's main purpose was to indulge the governor's passion for star-gazing. Enemies murmured that the tower allowed Merryweather to keep an eye specifically on the activities of women prisoners. Whatever the truth, the stunning view makes the steep climb worthwhile.

The bailey

The bailey

The 2.5-hectare (6-acre) area within the castle walls is known as the bailey. Today, as in previous years, it is used for a variety of purposes. The most colourful in the past was the tourney – a jousting event where knights on horseback with lances would endeavour to unseat each other at the gallop. Today re-enactments recapture some of the same medieval atmosphere.

The walls

One of the most enjoyable and spectacular parts of visiting the castle is to walk along the walls and savour the view. These were built in the early part of the 12th century to replace the original Norman timber walls, themselves constructed on top of a giant earth bank, up to 9 metres (30 feet) high and 25 metres (82 feet) broad.

The walls

The gaol

By the 18th century, the conditions in the castle's dungeons were so bad that in 1787 a new gaol was built to replace them. This was extended in 1847 on the lines of the Pentonville system then in vogue. The price which prisoners paid for the new, more sanitary, conditions was to have absolutely no contact with their fellow inmates. This is nowhere more evident than in the prison chapel with its separate stalls.

Lucy Tower

The tower was built in the 12th century by the formidable Lucy Taillebois, wife of Ranulph de Meschines, the Sheriff of Lincoln. Lucy was in charge while Ranulph was away, attending to his estates elsewhere, and she built the 15-sided tower in 1110 for herself and her soldiers. Eventually the tower fell into disrepair, and from 1829 the ground within became a graveyard for prisoners executed at the castle.

Lucy Tower

Bailgate

Bailgate takes you from Castle Hill to Newport Arch and beyond to the Museum of Lincolnshire Life and Ellis Mill. The area is known as the Bail, this being the castle's outer bailey – the defended area enclosed by its walls. Many of the houses hide within their cellars remains of the Roman settlement, which once had its centre here.

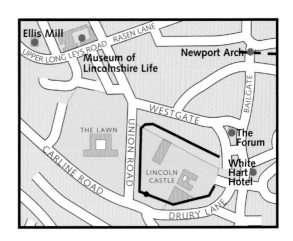

White Hart Hotel

Like most land and property in the Bail, the White Hart was once owned by the cathedral. It's thought to have been built around 1387, during the reign of King Richard II, whose emblem was a White Hart. In Tudor and Stuart times it became very dilapidated, and the earliest part of today's building dates from around 1710, when the hotel was reaching its peak as a coaching inn.

Forum

This was the hub of *Colonia Lindensium*, the walled Roman settlement established for retired legionaries in the upper part of the city. The stone forum was fronted by a magnificent colonnade – the positions of some columns are marked in the roadway. The forum contained an open square with walkways and statues, a basilica (town hall) and temples. Elsewhere were a theatre and baths.

Newport Arch

This arch, built in the 3rd century AD, is the most famous and best preserved of all Lincoln's Roman monuments. Through this gate legions left the upper city to begin their march north to York along Ermine Street. You can get a better idea of the level of the Roman road by looking at the level of the path that goes through the pedestrian arch.

Newport Arch

Phantom highwayman

The orangery in the White Hart Hotel was once a courtyard, where horse-drawn coaches would arrive and depart. It is said to be haunted by a phantom highwayman. On one occasion, when ordering a coach's passengers to 'stand and deliver', he received a flaming brand in his face. Horribly disfigured, he now searches for the coachman that wounded him.

Museum of Lincolnshire Life

This museum gives you a fascinating look at how Lincolnshire people lived in the past. Here you can wander through beautifully reconstructed rooms, domestic and commercial, and learn about the battle history of The Royal Lincolnshire Regiment, which ceased to be a separate unit in the 1960s. You can also see the sorts of vehicles and big machinery that Lincoln used to make. Pride of place goes of the world's first-ever tanks – Lincoln being the place where tanks were first invented and made.

Museum of Lincolnshire Life

Ellis Mill

Just behind the museum in Mill Road is this working windmill, the last of nine such mills that stood on the ridge. Run by volunteers, it is open at weekends in summer and on Sundays in winter. Here you can watch flour being ground, and even buy a good-value sample bag.

Ellis Mill

Lincoln Cathedral

To the outsider, Lincoln Cathedral is known as just that: a cathedral. Locally, though, it is spoken of as the Minster, a more accurate description. The title denotes a large church serving an area but which, unlike many cathedrals, was never a monastery. Founded in 1072 by Bishop Remigius, it was consecrated just after his death 20 years later. Its most important figure was Hugh of Grenoble, later St Hugh of Lincoln, who was bishop between 1186 and 1200. A man of boundless energy, he rebuilt the cathedral after an earthquake and defended the city's Jews against persecution.

The nave

In the early days of the Minster, the choir and chancel (the area between the screen and the high altar) tended to be for clergy and choir only. Traditionally free of seating, the nave was the public space, the place where pilgrims milled about, where people met, where plays and even markets were held. The black marble font from Tournai in Belgium symbolizes the beginning of the journey through life, a journey which ends at the Angel Choir with thoughts about death and the life hereafter.

The nave

Lincoln Imp

Although the cathedral authorities would perhaps prefer visitors' interest to focus on more angelic characters in the Minster, the Imp remains a continuing source of fascination. The tiny stone figure hides in the Angel Choir in the stonework above the shrine to St Hugh's head.

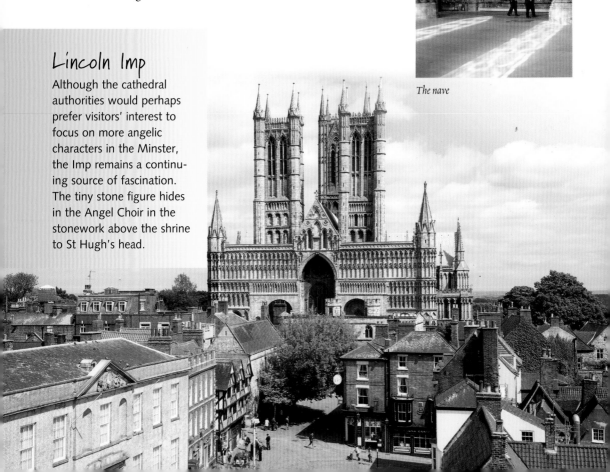

Bishop's Eye and Dean's Eye

At the end of each transept is a stunning circular stained-glass window, created in the 1220s. The Bishop's Eye, rebuilt in 1330, is over the south door, where medieval bishops entered the cathedral from the old palace. The Dean's Eye dominates the opposite transept, looking towards the Deanery.

South transept and Bishop's Eye

North transept and Dean's Eye

Chapter House

This spectacular ten-sided building is a masterpiece of medieval architecture and the first to be built in this style. Begun in the 1220s, it is still used for meetings of the General Chapter, the team of canons who administer the cathedral. During the 14th century, the English Parliament assembled here several times, while in 1536 participants of the Lincolnshire Uprising – a protest against Henry VIII's cynical style of Reformation – met here. Most were pardoned; some were hanged.

Angel Choir

Pilgrims flocked to the shrine of St Hugh, the great former bishop, after he died in 1200. By 1290 the cathedral had been extended at the east end to provide more space for these visitors. By October 1280 it was sufficiently complete for St Hugh's remains to be reinterred here in a ceremony witnessed by Edward I and Queen Eleanor. The angel sculptures within show the progression from earthly life via death to salvation in heaven. The Judgement Porch outside (see page 17) warns of the route to hell.

Chapter House vault

Minster Yard

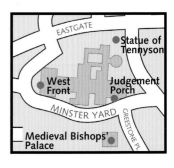

The Minster is the largest building within miles of Lincoln. Imagine the awe-inspiring effect that such a glorious, massive sight must have had on medieval folk who lived in tiny hovels. Indeed, the friezes over the two side doors were designed to bring the Bible to these people, most of whom could not read – Old Testament stories are on the left, New Testament on the right. The four so-called 'Number Houses' facing the Minster's west front were the first numbered houses in Lincoln. These dwellings are actually medieval in origin, but were renovated in the Georgian style in 1740.

West Front

The central portion, part of the 1092 Minster, is Romanesque in style, while the additions on either side are 13th-century Early English Gothic. The figure on top of the right-hand pinnacle is St Hugh of Lincoln. On the left is the 'Swineherd of Stow', a poor but generous man who gave money towards the building of the cathedral.

West Front

The dean's wife?

Look out on the right just past James Street and opposite the Deanery. From out of a wall on the right of Eastgate pops a single stone head. Some say it's the dean's wife checking he wasn't going to the old Swan public house. Others think it's the choirmaster checking on choristers late for practice.

Statue of Tennyson

Near the north-east corner of the cathedral is a statue of Alfred, Lord Tennyson (1809–92), the Poet Laureate famous for such poems as 'The Charge of the Light Brigade' and 'The Lady of Shalott', who was born in Somersby, Lincolnshire. This 1905 statue shows him with his wolfhound Karenina. Lincoln's Central Library and The Collection (see page 19) house Tennyson's papers and other memorabilia.

Statue of Tennyson

Judgement Porch

This porch is at the south-east corner of the Minster. It is full of hidden symbolism, the main theme being that hell is outside, heaven within; hence the boat above the statue of the Virgin and Child is sailing outward into hell. The famous Lincoln Imp is on board. To the right, near the corner of the church, are statues of Edward I and Queen Eleanor. The queen's entrails are interred in the Minster.

Medieval Bishops' Palace

In the Middle Ages, bishops had far more power than they do today – temporal as well as spiritual. Besides this, the Diocese of Lincoln was the second biggest in England, stretching from the Humber to the Thames. No wonder, then, that Lincoln's bishops lived in some splendour. The first palace, now a preserved ruin, was both a status symbol and a place to entertain important visitors.

Judgement Porch detail

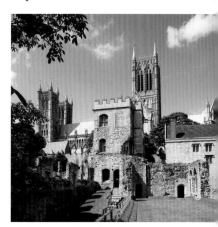

Medieval Bishops' Palace

Byrd and Swynford

Two celebrities of their day lived in Minster Yard. Katherine Swynford (1350–1403) was mistress, then wife, of John of Gaunt, Edward III's son and the most powerful nobleman in England. She is buried in the Minster. William Byrd (c.1540–1623) was organist and choirmaster at Lincoln, and one of the Elizabethan age's foremost composers and musicians.

Down the hill

Greestone Stairs and Lindum Road take you from Minster Yard back towards the commercial part of the city, past special spots that all afford peace and quiet in their different ways – a perfect antidote to the busyness you find elsewhere in the city.

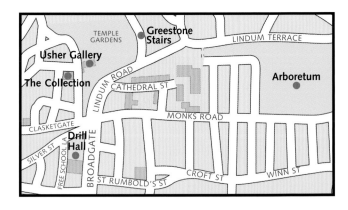

Temple Gardens

This attractive, peaceful hillside park was once a Victorian pleasure garden, where Roman fortifications and two medieval churches once stood. It was created by solicitor Joseph Moore in 1824 and residents paid an annual subscription to walk there. After Moore's death it fell into disrepair until bought by the city as a site for the Usher Gallery. The focus of the gardens is the Greek-style temple at the top.

Usher Gallery

Jeweller and watchmaker James Usher (1845–1921) amassed a wonderful collection of clocks, watches, ceramics and other items, which he left to the city with the money to build an art gallery and museum. Usher's pieces alone are worth a visit to the gallery, but there are also superb paintings of the area by important local artists such as Peter de Wint and William Logsdail. Look out for L.S. Lowry's picture of Lincoln. Apparently he needed a great deal of persuasion to include the cathedral!

Usher Gallery

The Collection

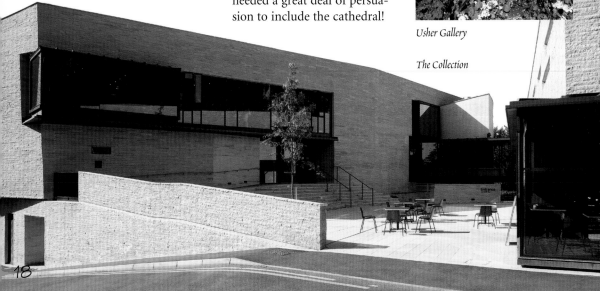

The Collection

The Collection

This superb museum, opened in 2005, is subtitled Art and Archaeology in Lincolnshire. The lofty, impressive building tells the county's history through artefacts and displays. In particular, don't miss the 2,500-year-old dug-out canoe, many examples of Roman pavements and pottery, and a giant aerial map of the county. Besides the permanent display, temporary touring exhibitions are featured.

The Arboretum

The Arboretum is a magical park, opened in 1872 on the eastern slopes of the city and beautifully restored in 2003. Designed by Edward Milner, who once served as an apprentice to Chatsworth's famous

Sir Joseph Paxton, it has several special features, notably the Arboretum Terrace, a lovely tree-lined walk; a 19th-century rose garden; a delightful lake with fountains; and an intriguing maze.

Lincoln Drill Hall

This was the headquarters of the 4th Battalion Lincolnshire Regiment, and was built for the city in 1890 by Joseph Ruston, a local industrialist who made famous agricultural machinery and excavators. It was once known as the 'bread and cheese hall' after Ruston said that his workers' wage demands would leave him eating only bread and cheese. It is now a community arts venue.

The Arboretum

Waterside and waterfront

Lincoln's waterside areas provide an attractive breathing space in the city's busiest area. Riverside paths take full advantage of this, making an hour by the water a must for anyone visiting the city. You can enjoy a walk along Lincoln's waterside paths in any direction.

Waterside

Where the Waterside Shopping Centre (built 1987–91) now stands was originally marshy ground, which the Romans reclaimed, building piers and creating inlets. Here Stephen Broadbent's *Empowerment* sculpture spans the River Witham from City Square. Its theme is God empowering mankind in the form of Adam. Privately funded, the sculpture reflects the city's engineering heritage.

Brayford Pool

Brayford Pool is where the River Witham joins the Fossdyke, the canal built by the Romans (using the former River Till) to link Lincoln with the River Trent. This conjunction of important roads and waterways meant that the pool, once much larger than it is today, became the focus of prosperous waterborne trade, especially in wool and corn. Warehouses were built on reclaimed land around its sides and local industry boomed. However, in the 20th century the area went into steep decline. Now, thanks to Lincoln University, it has taken on a new life.

Waterside North and Empowerment sculpture

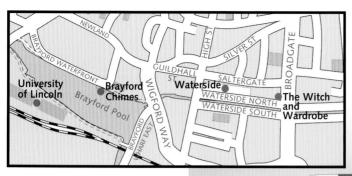

University of Lincoln

Until the 1990s the scene here was one of decay and desolation. William Foster's testing ground nearby had long since seen its last tank rumble away (see page 3). What had once been bustling railway sidings and goods sheds were wasteland by the early 1960s. Now this fine university campus, opened in 1996, has been at the heart of Brayford Pool's renaissance, helping to give the city a new identity in this post-industrial age.

University of Lincoln

Brayford Waterchimes

Created by Andy Plant in 2001, this sculpture is continually on the move, falling water being used to strike the hour. However, the clock's mechanical record has been rather unreliable, so don't be surprised if you find it dry.

Mute swans

Brayford Pool is known for its mute swans. Australian black swans can occasionally be seen, too. Don't be tempted to feed them, however. In the past well-meaning onlookers have threatened the flock's survival by giving them the wrong sort of food.

Brayford Pool

The Witch and Wardrobe

This restored 15th-century building by Broadgate Bridge is reputed to be haunted. Originally it was a high-class brothel serving gentry from the castle, and from that era come two young lovers occasionally seen or heard upstairs. There's also Tommy, a mischievous but highly sensitive poltergeist, who has been known to shake the plates on the wall violently when he's upset.

Around the Lincoln area

Although it's mainly the county town itself that draws visitors to Lincolnshire, there is certainly no shortage of interesting places to visit in the surrounding area, from Second World War airfields to the little known beauty of the Lincolnshire Wolds.

Doddington Hall

Doddington Hall

This is a wonderful late Elizabethan mansion, just beyond the city's western outskirts. It comes complete with walled courtyards, romantic gardens and a gabled gatehouse. What makes Doddington special is that it has remained in the same family since it was built in 1600. This 400-year story is reflected in its beautiful textiles, porcelain, furniture and paintings.

RAF Scampton

Lincolnshire was the wartime home of many bomber squadrons and is still dotted with active air bases. Nearest to Lincoln is RAF Scampton, 4 miles (6 kilometres) north of the city. The RAF Aerobatic Team, the 'Red Arrows', is based here. Tours of the base and its museum are available by appointment only.

A 'Red Arrow' at RAF Scampton

Tealby

Lincolnshire Wolds

These lovely chalky uplands run south from the Humber Estuary parallel to the coast. A designated Area of Outstanding Natural Beauty, they are one of Britain's best-kept secrets, offering spectacular views from open hilltops and

Horncastle

The Wolds market town of Horncastle, like Lincoln, has a Roman past. Little evidence of this remains visible, but in compensation there are many delightful 18th and 19th-century buildings and a superb array of antique shops to browse among.

Horncastle

The Tennyson connection

Alfred Lord Tennyson was born in 1809 at Somersby in the Wolds, where his father was Rector. His father's brother Charles was the arrogant squire of Tealby who, despite being left all

the family money, resented Alfred's success, branding his poetry 'horrid rubbish … a discredit to British taste'. Tennyson is also linked to Harrington Hall (home of a girlfriend, Rosa Baring) and Tetford, near Horncastle, where for a while the poet was a regular at the White Hart Inn – Dr Johnson, too, but in a different era.

Mrs Smith's Cottage

Hilda Smith was 102 when she died in 1995. Now, the little brick cottage in Navenby where she lived for more than 70 years has been lovingly preserved just as she left it. What makes it even more special is that Mrs Smith kept a detailed diary of every aspect of her life. Her personality lives on in every tiny corner of her cottage, which is open to the public most days. Navenby is 9 miles (14 kilometres) south of Lincoln on the A607.

Mrs Smith and her cottage

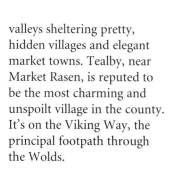

valleys sheltering pretty, hidden villages and elegant market towns. Tealby, near Market Rasen, is reputed to be the most charming and unspoilt village in the county. It's on the Viking Way, the principal footpath through the Wolds.

Around the Lincoln area

Stamford

Although Stamford is a good hour's drive to the south of Lincoln, it is certainly worth the journey. It is a remarkable Georgian town, very popular with visitors and, as a peaceful time-capsule, it is often featured in period films and dramas. It also has lovely views of the River Welland and nearby is Burghley House, the magnificent Elizabethan mansion built by Lord Burghley.

Belvoir Castle

Woodhall Spa

Two curiosities hide in this pretty town, once an Edwardian watering place, 15 miles (24 kilometres) or so south-east of Lincoln. Petwood House Hotel was a wartime RAF Officer's Mess, and the Squadron Bar here has all sorts of memorabilia from 617 Squadron, the 'Dambusters' led by Guy Gibson. Close by is the 'Kinema in the Woods', a delightful old-style picture house which has changed little since 1922. On summer afternoons it often shows nostalgia films, which casual visitors are very welcome to watch too.

Belvoir Castle

This famous stately home near Grantham, seat of the Dukes of Rutland, has starred in many films. It is Norman in origin but was remodelled in the 19th century by James Wyatt and is now very popular with visitors, both for the building with its works of art and for the delightful grounds.

Stamford

RAF Coningsby

RAF Coningsby

This active airfield, 20 miles (32 kilometres) south-east of Lincoln, is notable as the home of the Battle of Britain Memorial Flight. The Flight comprises an Avro Lancaster, two Hurricanes, a Dakota, five Spitfires, and two Chipmunks, which can

Sir Isaac Newton's birthplace

You'll remember that famous scientist Sir Isaac Newton was inspired to discover the principle of gravity by watching an apple fall from a tree. He did this at his birthplace, Woolsthorpe Manor in Woolsthorpe-by-Colsterworth, a village near Grantham. Now owned by the National Trust, this fine stone yeoman's house is open to visitors each year from spring to autumn.

Tattershall Castle

be viewed during the week in guided tours. The exhibition centre is also open on most weekdays. Tattershall Castle is close by and it is also well worth visiting.

Southwell, Nottinghamshire

This is England's smallest 'cathedral town' with attractive streets and unusual shops. The town is profusely decked out in summer

Southwell Minster

with hanging baskets. The Norman Minster, with its distinctive western towers, is unspoilt Romanesque in its architecture: massive round pillars and rounded arches. Don't miss the Workhouse on the eastern fringe of the town. Superbly restored by the National Trust, an audio guide talks you through how things were for the poor in 1840 who were left with nowhere else to go.

Information

What's on
Check with the Visitor Information Centre for full and up-to-date information on all events.

January
Australian breakfast

March
Discover Lincoln Weekend

May
Music Live: procession of drummers from the castle to City Square, venue for live music acts of many types

June
Lincolnshire Show;
Midsummer Magic;
Open-air concerts in the castle grounds;
RAF Waddington Air Show

July
Brayford Waterfront Festival;
Medieval Weekend: costumed medieval dramas performed in the castle grounds;
Summer Food Fair, Castle Square

August
Midsummer Magic: open-air concerts in the castle grounds;
Lincolnshire Steam & Vintage Rally, County Showground on A15

September
Heritage Open Days: county-wide walks, talks, open buildings, special events

December
Christmas Market, Castle Hill (see page 9)

i **The Lincoln Visitor Information Centre**
9 Castle Hill
Lincoln LN1 3AA
tel: 01522 545458
email: visitorinformation@lincolnbig.co.uk
website:
www.visitlincolnshire.com

Shopmobility
For the use of powered wheelchairs and scooters for those with limited mobility. Based at Melville Street Bus Station
Mon–Sat 9.00–12.00 and 13.00–16.30.
To book, tel: 01522 514477

Theatre Royal
The Theatre Royal in Clasketgate is an Edwardian former music hall. These days it presents everything from operas, musicals and concerts to local shows and pantomimes. You have only to sit in the auditorium to sample the amazing and nostalgic atmosphere.

Christmas Market

Walk and Ride bus service

This minibus service operates in Lincoln city centre every day except Christmas Day and Boxing Day. Buses run every 20 minutes in a circular route from 10 a.m. to 5 p.m. Monday to Saturday, and from 12 noon on Sunday. The bus links up with all the main carparks, coach stops, and the bus and railway stations.

Lincoln attractions

The Collection – Art and Archaeology 01522 550990, www.thecollection.lincoln.museum;
Ellis Mill 01522 528448;
Museum of Lincolnshire Life 01522 528448, www.lincolnshire.gov.uk/ museumoflincolnshirelife;
Lincoln Castle 01522 511068, www.lincolnshire.gov.uk/lincolncastle;
Lincoln Cathedral 01522 561600, www.lincolncathedral.com;
Lincoln Drill Hall 01522 873894, www.lincolndrillhall.com;
Lincoln Guildhall 01522 873507, www.lincoln.gov.uk;
Medieval Bishops' Palace 01522 527468, www.English-heritage.org.uk;
Theatre Royal 01522 525555 or 519999, www.theatreroyallincoln.com

Around Lincoln:

Doddington Hall 01522 694308, www.doddingtonhall.com;
Battle of Britain Memorial Flight Visitor Centre, RAF Coningsby 01526 344041, www.bbmf.co.uk;
Gainsborough Old Hall 01427 612669;
Lincolnshire Aviation Heritage Centre 01790 763207, www.lincsaviation.co.uk;
Mrs Smith's Cottage 01529 414294, www.oden.co.uk/mrssmith;
Tattershall Castle, near Horncastle 01526 342543, www.nationaltrust.org.uk

Tours and trips

The Visitor Information Centre has details of all tours and trips.

Green Badge guides lead walking tours from the VIC at Castle Hill daily during the summer.

Ghost walks also take small groups around the cathedral and castle all year round beginning at 7p.m. in Castle Hill.

Two companies run boat trips on the River Witham and the Fossdyke, starting from Brayford Waterfront.

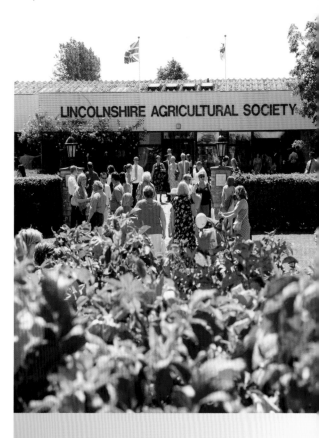

Lincolnshire Show

The county's biggest event is held at the County Showground north of the city on A15. Here you will see farm animals, crafts, food and other displays.

Front cover:
Lincoln Cathedral
Back cover:
Leigh-Pemberton House,
Castle Hill

Acknowledgements

Photography © Pitkin Publishing
by Neil Jinkerson.
Additional photography by
kind permission of: Alamy 24t
(BL Images Ltd), 25 (Matthew
Richardson); Crown Copyright
25t; Doddington Hall 22t;
Friends of Mrs Smith's Cottage
23br; Lincoln Cathedral 14tr,
15 all; Lincolnshire Agricultural
Society 27; Lincolnshire County
Council 19t, 26; John McIlwain
16br, 19bl, 22br, 25cr.

The publishers would like to
thank Veronica Carchedi, the
staffs of Lincoln VIC, Lincoln
Castle and Lincoln Cathedral,
and Green Badge guide Arthur
Hazeldine for their assistance in
the preparation of this guide.

Written by John McIlwain; the
author has asserted his moral
rights.
Edited by Angela Royston.
Designed by Simon Borrough.
Additional picture research by
Jan Kean.
City map by The Map Studio,
Romsey, Hants, UK; walk maps
by Simon Borrough; maps based
on cartography © Ordnance
Survey.

© Crown copyright and/or
database right 2007. All rights
reserved. License number
100017593

Publication in this form © Pitkin
Publishing 2007, latest reprint
2010.
No part of this publication may
be reproduced by any means
without the permission of Pitkin
Publishing and the copyright
holders.

All information correct at time
of going to press, but may be
subject to change.

Printed in Great Britain.
ISBN 978-1-84165-199-6   2/10

PITKIN CITY GUIDES

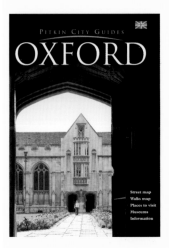
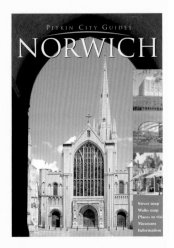

This guide is just one in a series of city titles

Available by mail order
See our website, **www.pitkin-guides.com**, for our full range
of titles, or contact us for a copy of our brochure.

Pitkin Publishing, Healey House, Dene Road, Andover,
Hampshire, SP10 2AA, UK
Sales and enquiries: 01264 409200
Fax: 01264 334110
Email: sales@thehistorypress.co.uk